bathtub in flames.

bathtub in flames.

Bailee Noella

New Degree Press
Copyright © 2020 Bailee Noella
All rights reserved.

bathtub in flames.

ISBN	978-1-63676-511-2	*Paperback*
	978-1-63676-035-3	*Kindle Ebook*
	978-1-63676-036-0	*Ebook*

Dedicated to my younger self.

Contents

note from the author. 13
anesthesiologist. 16

the things that steal our parents. 17
kids in summer. 18
sorry, but i have to. 19
my very short list. 20
knee-scraper. 22
it rains somewhere. 24
driftwood. 26
creaky floorboards. 27
bread crumbs. 29
hook, line, and sinker. 30
yoga in the driveway. 32
the dress in your closet. 34
atlas. 36
what she doesn't know may hurt her. 38
from a string, from a thread. 39
cicadas. 40
pilot error. 43
muted tv. 44
you never finished writing that song about me. 46

the right idea.	47
bukowski.	48
the sink, an ash tray.	50
february.	51
ceiling fan.	52
the difference between au revoir and adieu.	53
world's shortest, dullest autobiography.	55
co2.	56
i got bay leaves tattooed on my wrist because i'm a sentimental piece of shit.	57
interlude.	59
defibrillation.	61
last night in noblesville.	63
ok fine i miss you.	64
middle names.	66
half-regrets.	67
veracity.	68
all the words that end in -mania.	69
pyrrhic victory.	70
note in chicago.	71
the last time i smoked.	72
empty church parking lot.	73
vestigial responses.	74
l*ve and its tendencies.	75
dissipate I.	77
dissipate II.	78
thoughts from the foot of my bed.	79
agnostic.	80
i used to call my mom by her first name.	81
love you more, love you most.	82
unorthodox genie.	83
is it considered minimalistic if i just want you?	84
(sorry, i know you hate spiders.)	85

numbers divisible by three.	86
reversing amnesia.	87
matryoshkas.	89
the corner of the room where my demon appears.	90
a conversation between survivors.	92
cinderblock.	93
tiny.	97
blanket hoarding.	98
bathtub in flames.	99
strangulation.	101
how i wish the conversation would go.	102
the pause.	104
on humans and addiction.	105
posthumous apology.	106
our souls as sponges.	107
water over white stones.	109
neon turmoil.	111
empty buckets for eyes.	112
day two hundred ten.	113
past the popcorn ceiling.	114
beacon park drive.	116
fearless as the sand.	118
cataracts.	119
grow up!	121
telephone poles.	122
reruns.	123
120 bpm.	124
the cycle.	125
catharsis.	126
be patient.	128
acknowledgments.	131

*Maybe you are searching among the branches
for what only appears in the roots.*

—RUMI

TRIGGER WARNING.

Many poems in this collection deal with potentially triggering topics, including but not limited to mental illness, alcoholism, and self-harm. Please be aware of this as you read.

In order to make this collection more accessible for survivors of sexual abuse, poems containing direct mention or the allusion of such abuse have a separator between the title and the poem.

note from the author.

"What's your earliest memory?"

My friend asked me this a few years ago. We were leaning against a metal rail that overlooked the White River in downtown Indianapolis. It was the middle of summer, but the night was cool and crisp. A breeze bit at our uncovered arms and combed through our hair.

I told her that I couldn't pinpoint anything exactly. There were some fuzzy, blurry-around-the-edges images that came to mind of me as a child—snapshots of early birthday parties, petting reindeer, toppling from a kitchen chair—but nothing concrete. My memories seemed to start, I told her, from when I was around thirteen.

The shock on her face made me realize something that I had always known but never wanted to question: It was odd that the first decade or so of my life was almost entirely missing from my memory. I might as well have spilled a cartridge of black ink over my childhood.

Logically, I knew that I had not fallen from the sky and appeared at my parents' doorstep as an angst-filled teen. There was an entire past—a whole person—that I was missing out on. I wanted to know myself and all of my depths; I vowed to find my childhood self, even though I knew there were sinister reasons I was unable to remember her.

After several gut-wrenching years of digging, the pieces started to fall into place—countless hours of therapy, flipping through family photo albums, requesting medical records, and horrible nightmares. I knew a lot of the anxiety I had stuffed inside me was thanks to a tumultuous childhood, but I never expected the memories of sexual abuse that resurfaced.

My life fell apart for a while after that. The flashbacks took my body with a ferocity, almost as if they were enraged I had awoken them, and I found myself wishing I had never excavated this other trauma that my inner child had never gotten the chance to heal from. There were many nights I found myself showering repeatedly, trying to wash away what I knew had happened, and there were days I lashed out at anyone who touched me. I wanted to shove the memories back down inside me, deep in a pocket of my brain where they could never crawl out again, but once they had reached the surface, they refused to be ignored again.

As the years trudged on, quietly and with a softness, the pain began to melt—and it never evaporated, not fully. But as I held and spoke to my inner child, it did grow dull. And I'm grateful for it in a way that I couldn't have been when the memories first arose; I'm thankful to know where the pain stems from so that I may take care of myself the way I deserved to be taken care of as a kid.

These poems chronicle the journey toward remembering my childhood and the years it took to recover. I hope that, as you read this collection of poems, you are able to see yourself in them as I have found myself in them while writing.

anesthesiologist.

i have always had a hand that aches to write,
to find a companion in this feeling.

i often find myself waiting for something to rush at me
and even more often retiring to bed

without having written
anything at all.

still, there is a sense of urgency about it,
like i have a letter to mail off and very limited time to send it.

the thing about writing
is that sometimes you don't know who you're writing to,

you just hope it gets to them on time.

the things that steal our parents.

even a child could see
you were searching in the wrong places—
there were empty bottles and
terrible men that stayed for many nights;
i would have saved you if you'd let me,
if ever that was a possibility.
you slipped down dark alleys of sleep
like you didn't have appointments to go to
or cats and kids to feed.
there was a time i thought
i was to blame for your
forgetting my existence,
thought you throwing rosaries
and shouting obscenities
was my fault and no one else's,
but i know now that you simply
belonged to whatever tyrant
ruled your splintered head.
and once it sank its teeth in,
i saw you everyday
but never again.

kids in summer.

i can't remember where we were heading
only that we were going there fast

and our popsicles were melting
and the soles of our feet were dirty

i can't remember why we were laughing
only that we got lost in it

and our dinner was getting cold
and our parents were calling

and nothing seemed to matter.

sorry, but i have to.

will i see you again?
i asked, already wishing i hadn't.

she sat back, spine flush
against the trunk of the oak,
toes curling against its roots
as if to anchor herself to the world,
to keep from drifting away before she meant to.

i don't know, she replied
and her voice tiptoed right past me;
i could barely hear the frail thing.

i couldn't bear to crumple in front of her,
so i looked instead at the playground
and the lighters littered on the mulch.

she plucked the loose strings on her jeans,
inhaled so sharply i thought she might hurt herself,
and made a horrible, twisted request:

please try not to write about me.

my very short list.

i plop a stool down in the kitchen,
creaky worn wood that i
climb on top of,
and drag a pencil across the ceiling,
make it look like there are cracks,
like the roof might cave in.
i recall
my list, my so-very-short list
of things that i miss:

you you you

i start to sing it:

you you you

feel horrible, ridiculous
tumbling
from the stool onto
the tile floor into
the saddest most pathetic part
of my timid mind. i think
maybe i will sell
my fridge or
my apartment or
my button collection,
buy a plane ticket to the other side
so i can come see

you
you
you

knee-scraper.

***

i used to intentionally scrape my knees
just to see the neighbor kid.

i tumbled from my bike every chance i got,
and he pointed out my bloody elbows every time i rode to
    his house,

one hand still gripping the coke can i brought him,
the other outstretched for the two quarters he owed me.

another fall? he would pout,
pulling a tattered bandaid from his pocket

i would smile sheepishly
and watch him stick it to my skin.

it meant a lot back then
to have a boy checking up on me

when my father and brothers
couldn't, didn't,

and when the only other men in my life
were molesting me.

the last time i saw him was a week
before my family was due to move.

hey there, knee-scraper, he said
how many scabs today?

i hoped i had
enough to last awhile—

quite a few,
i told him.

no problem, he said
wiping the blood from my legs.

i didn't tell him
i was moving away

or that i had fallen as hard as i could
before coming to see him—

no problem, he said
wiping the tears from my face.

it rains somewhere.

you never came to me
when you were crying—
that broke my heart a little.

when i told you,
you laughed. asked
if the sky was obligated
to inform me every time
it rained somewhere.

you asked for space
so i gave it to you;
you told me to listen to your words,
not the grip that tightened around my hand
when i stood to leave.

you phoned me early
one april morning, laughing
because your car was breaking down
on the side of the road,
and so were you—

you said you were tired of searching,
it was driving you insane.
said something about
hitchhiking to the edge of the earth
to question god himself.

i wondered where you were,
told you i was coming and to go nowhere,
and you asked me if it gets better.
part of the tragedy, i suppose,
is that i couldn't bring myself to lie.

driftwood.

you drifted far,
out of arms reach.
so far that nothing could bring you back.
not an "i love you"
or an embrace
or me staying up all night
with you.

i tried, i swear i tried
but you never heard me
and finally a day came when
it was too late,
when the waves swallowed you whole
and never gave you back.

you used to stare at the moon
longingly for someone
who had never been there

i hope you're there now.

creaky floorboards.

i know sometimes you wish we could talk again,
and i'm sorry that i make you wait.

really, i'm sorry
to anyone who has ever loved me,

a distant and clingy in-between kind of creature,
infatuated with not trying and trying too hard.

it's just—you have to understand—
i grew up surrounded by
a lot of yelling for no reason, yelling
for so long i had to pretend not to exist to survive it,
and i still tense when anyone raises their voice.

i learned which creaky floorboards to avoid
like i learned which nights to avoid you.

there were nights with cops and nights i
could hardly reach the pedal but had to drive;
there were nights i wasn't sure you would ever
make it home safe
and nights i felt it might be better if
you didn't—
i'm sorry.

nothing could save me from
the pain of loving you,
except to love you harder and
from a distance.

i know sometimes you wish we could talk again,
and i'm sorry—really sorry—

but you'll have to wait.

bread crumbs.

i floated above and
around you
while you spoke.
you said that
i never gave enough,
that you wanted more of me.

i hadn't been the same
lately, and you wanted to know why.
called me ungrateful,
selfish;
told me i only ever
gave you bread crumbs.

i hoped i might fall
through the floor,
fall until i hit
the earth's core and
could be reborn again
as someone
who didn't have to give
when bread crumbs were all i had.

the half of me
still left
crawled into your arms
and prayed to die—

be happy to hold what you can.

hook, line, and sinker.

your hands never fully
grasp things. there are dips and
valleys in your palms
that make it impossible.

still,
i woke up at 7:22
on a sunday
to see if i could find
god again; i had to
conquer mountains of
unwashed clothes
to escape the bedroom.

then there was the dog,
and i had to have breakfast,
return some calls,
mom wanted to talk—

i showed up late to mass,
that inborn catholic guilt
built up again,
i had to walk past
dozens of perfect people
to find an open pew.

then there was the service,
and i had to stand then kneel,
find prayers in the book,
shake hands and offer peace—

but your hands never fully
grasp things. there are dips and
valleys in your palms
that make it impossible. and
we all exist in that space,
gaping and grasping
at things we can never really hold,
lying at rock bottom
looking to invisible beings
to convince us to stay
because nothing in the distance
between our bodies
and the rest of the world
does the trick.

yoga in the driveway.

we're standing in the driveway
i see your mouth moving but
i don't know what's coming out.
i apologize and
ask you to repeat yourself,
so you repeat yourself:

something about how
mom's totaled her car again
something about
more jail time,
but i don't catch it all.

oh.
oh, okay.

i think about the times i
begged her not to leave the house;
i knew she was drunk but still she got in
the car, and i didn't know it yet,
but i would carry that guilt with me
forever.

i stare at a blade of grass
wishing desperately
that i could trade places with it,
spend the rest of my life being neatly trimmed
and accepting the wind without a fight.

are you alright? you ask,
but i feel like vomiting
every time i remember my childhood
so i lay down
in the driveway—
shavasana,
the corpse pose—

i'm fine.

the dress in your closet.

those memories
still steal your breath sometimes—
at night, at coffee shops,
in the middle of meetings.

i know you'd like to pretend,
for your brother's sake,
that the past and those photographs
don't bother you.

when your brows knit together
and you begin to sob—
loud, gasping, chest-rattling sobs—
what can i do
except hold you?

what can i do
except lay with you and hope
that you give it a little more time,
that you let the light
warm your face
in the morning?

i know

the dress you wore to his funeral
takes up space in your closet and your heart

i'm sorry

the universe doesn't care
that it was too soon for you.

atlas.

british indie wafted from the car speakers
climbing out the cracked windows,
into the stillness of the unlit parking lot.

we sat in those leather seats hours after you'd gotten off work
separated only by the center console
and our dwindling willpower.

the song waned and we were encased in silence
both looking at the flickering lamp posts
because we were too smart to look at each other.

i almost said something stupid, you confessed.

earth never holds her breath
except to eavesdrop on love
and she happened to hold her breath then—

it hit me, suddenly
the pain of discussing love
when it wasn't an option.

the pain of holding the weight of the world
and the weight of knowing
why we turned our heads when we embraced.

don't say it, i told you.
just let me know
when you get home safe.

and because that was all we had—
the closest we could get—
you smiled, sat back, said

you too.

what she doesn't know may hurt her.

he wore his love like i wear my freckles
in plain sight but sort of seasonal

he called at three in the morning
to tell me he was in my ice-covered driveway

and we snuck out to the drugstore
for painkillers and some fresh air

he talked about his first car, how he crashed it
and said that if the wreck had happened in slow motion

it would have felt a lot like loving you.

from a string, from a thread.

he had photos of you still
strung up on the living room wall
the first time he found the audacity
to have me over.
yellowing, hanging from a string,
from a thread,
like the two of you.
i had to bring
all of the world's oxygen
into my chest
to keep from saying anything.
he bunched the photos up,
calloused knuckles quivering, said:
don't need these anymore.
but there was no hiding how
it shook him to ball up your face
and destroy any evidence
of your time together.
i slid my shoes off and
trekked upstairs without a word,
already pulling my shirt over my head
and pretending he didn't still
deeply need you;
i wish i had connected
the dots then, but i was eighteen
not much made sense and
i would have given my life
if it meant an ounce
of love.

cicadas.

***

how was it?
he asks me
with a five-star grin on his face,
collecting my tights from the floor
and tossing them my way.

i force a smile,
all cheek and no heart—
i'd grown up doing that—
and pull them back on,
sitting, reeling
on the edge of his mattress.

i try to form an answer,
something that will
stroke his ego so
he'll keep me around
for a few more months,
maybe a year if i'm lucky,
but nothing comes to mind;

that feeling of being robbed
sneaks back into my chest again,
that sickness as all the times
i've ever been touched
come rushing back to me
and i grow nauseous.

how was it?
he pushes;
it's only a question
but i want to slap him for it,
for all the men who ever
took from me and
were never sorry.

he tilts his head
at my silence—
how was it?
how was it?
how was it?—
i can't bear to look at his face,
the face of someone
who isn't reminded of
something sinister
every time he is touched,
who just has sex and dies
like cicadas do
and doesn't mind.

the nausea grows
and grows so
i gather my feet and
escape his bed,
stumble to the bathroom,
toss the door open and
slump over the toilet,

ready to vomit up the memories
until i can act unbothered again.

i kneel there for quite some time,
half-praying to die on the spot
and never see another man again,
half-wondering if i want to hide in sex
or if i am disgusted it exists,
twirling in that whirlwind of uncertainty
only survivors know.

i hear him clear his throat
outside the door,
shuffling his ego
between his feet;
he knocks lightly
as i throw up in his bathroom:
was it that bad?

pilot error.

your hair was tousled and rowdy;
i was proud of it
and as you got cleaned up,
it hurt a little to watch you
erase the evidence of love on the sidelines of
your bed.
company came over,
friends from california
and even farther, i was introduced and then
forgotten. all of them sat in
a circle, passing blunts and judgments.
i couldn't help eyeing you from the corner,
admiring the way the heavy smoke
blurred your face, morphing you
into a monet painting
with psychedelic traces of van gogh.
you met my sleepy gaze,
eyes dancing with drunkenness and
looking ready to cause me a great deal
of heartache. i should've known it then,
should've laced my superstars and run
for miles in the opposite direction,
but i've never been too good about
catching myself before i fall,
and it's a shame that you were
such a hard landing.

muted tv.

the sheets shift, like a moth taking flight;
a sound only a decibel above his escapee heart

his warmth maneuvers closer to the window,
dust-ridden and seeping cold.

i can hardly fathom how hard i must be to love
if sleeping beside cracked glass is more appealing.

i fumble for my car keys, find my socks and some leftover dignity
sit on the edge of his tattered mattress and feel consumed
    by the lack of love,

consumed by nothing at all.

most nights i would stay and curl up against his hollow form
try to radiate life into him, and love, and all the other
    things he turned his back on

i'd stay and splay my palm across his chest, pitiful and concaving,
marvel at the emptiness there and wish i were enough to
    fill it.

i'd stay, press quaking lips to still spine,
and tell him i love him 'til he pushed me away,

muting me like the tv
so he could get some sleep.

you never finished writing that song about me.

i stole the still-lit cigarette from between your teeth,

packed my feelings for you tightly between tobacco

and tossed it onto the pavement, stifled it beneath my shoe

i hate you, i said

you pulled a lighter out from your sweatpants pocket,

and i cursed god for gifting you with steady hands

well, you replied, sparking up, *it's about fucking time.*

the right idea.

i woke up early one morning
and went out to your back porch,

sat beside the cinnamon-colored flower pot
you abused as an ashtray

and watched your neighbors
yell and toss memorabilia over their balcony.

heart-shaped vases and thrifted sweaters
rained over the yellowing lawn

until the well of valentine's day gifts ran dry
and they threatened to force each other over the ledge.

the elderly woman from next door stepped outside,
tsked at me over the top of the rusted grill she used as a
    fence

and motioned to the wrestling couple with a veiny hand.
they're both fucking crazy, huh? she said.

well, i replied, following her gaze with a grin,
i think they might be onto something.

bukowski.

my boy is on the futon
flicking his tongue across a redhead's teeth,
making awful sounds
and worse faces.
i feel terribly betrayed, but worse

i can't find the bathroom—

i stumble around,
drunk and wanting to die a little,
or maybe just to sleep into my late thirties.

i wonder if bukowski would've loved me;
we could've gotten married in the kitchen
and i wouldn't have to invite my mother
or scramble to make plans
and there wouldn't be any contracts involved,
the way love ought to be.

but no one answers me
when i ask them if bukowski would've loved me
or when i ask them where the bathroom is,

so i stagger over to the window
for a breath of fresh air and to imagine jumping out of it,
naturally

the wooden frame as splintered as my breathing;
i look out at the city below, above, all around,
surrounding me
until i grow sick,
grow dizzy and nauseous and furious:

there are billions of people in the world
and not a single one of them
could love you into
a good man.

the sink, an ash tray.

we shared that sink
every morning and
every night;

it was a cramped little bathroom
stuffed full of your cigarette smoke
where we got ready for bed together

i'd step aside so you could
brush your teeth, and you'd watch me
pull my hair into a bun.

you told me i looked cute with my
hair up; that's when
i should have known you were a liar.

i remember one night,
toward the end, when you said
i love you—

not because you meant it but
just to try it on.
and i said it back, relieved

to finally have something in common
with your mother.

february.

it was some night in the middle of february
when i saw her silhouette in your bedroom window

i stood there, ankle-deep in snow,
with a useless key in hand and my breath in the air

numb and shaking in your stupid jacket,
but not because of the cold.

i figured the most hurtful thing i could do in return
was pretend you never existed,

so i turned my back to that red brick apartment,
ditched your jacket, and drove home.

now that years have gone by
i no longer hope for an apology;

i just hope, for your sake and hers,
that you've grown a pair.

ceiling fan.

your name is engraved in my ceiling fan
six letters etched with a heavy hand
and liberally embellished with fool's gold
like every word that came out of your mouth

maybe i'll carve your name
into the door frame, too
and into the passenger seat
and into my wistful palms

i wouldn't feel much different if i did
you're everywhere anyway
in cold windy nights at the drive thru
and smoke-filled rooms and black futons

i still wake up
empty-handed and detoxing
considering a smaller mattress
and staring at my ceiling fan

was something always missing
or did you create the space?

the difference between au revoir and adieu.

the blue marches into my bedroom
the way dads do when you're
late for school.
i roll out of bed, groggy,
hair messy;
roll onto the floor with my
feet useless beneath me.
my cheek against the rough threads,
i count the strands in my carpet—
i still need to vacuum—
count them the way i
used to count the hair on your head.
count and then lose count and
start to cry;
this is my morning ritual,
only it's late afternoon.
i'm lazy and useless and
there's this rift between
my rib cages,
a divide even deeper and wider
and less fixable than the one
between us. but
it's not the distance
that paralyzes me,
it's that you said

au revoir

when you meant

adieu.

world's shortest, dullest autobiography.

i started crying inside of a gas station once:
jackie blue was playing over the speakers
it was past midnight
and i was searching the fridges for yoo-hoo

there's something about '70s music
and childish chocolate drinks
something about randomly recalling the divorce rate
i just lost it

i went to the counter,
pointed to a pack of marlboro reds, and
the cashier handed them to me without asking for my i.d.,
without asking why i was crying.

i had to wonder which was worse:
actively seeking a nicotine addiction,
or knowing i would pussy out
before i could figure out which end goes in my mouth

i walked back through the automatic doors feeling
unloved by myself,
unloved by the universe,
and certainly unloved by the ricker's cashier.

co2.

trying to put you in the back of my mind
hurts
like holding smoke in my lungs
and i hope i can exhale you
before you kill me.

i got bay leaves tattooed on my wrist because i'm a sentimental piece of shit.

i was an avalanche, falling from the driver's seat one
    afternoon
spilling onto the unforgiving floor of my garage

bones on fire, and some aching beneath my skin—
pains that had always been present

my cheek pressed hard against the cement
and my chest too tight for my tachycardia

i remember crying—
a lot of crying—

and wishing the tires of my camry would deflate,
that physics would bend for all three tons of it to topple
    onto me.

i don't remember how i stood up, or how long it took
to drag me and my self-pity into the kitchen

i don't remember grabbing my take-out bowl of soup from
the passenger seat,
only that it was there when i reached the table.

what a talented multitasker i am, i thought,
eating chicken noodle, and crying, and contemplating
    suicide!

the next spoonful i lifted to my lips
there was the tiniest bay leaf, smaller than my pinky nail

it was the cutest and funniest thing i had ever seen
a leaf, that small and lonesome, swimming around in
   my bowl—

i absolutely lost my shit.

it's so miniscule and
it doesn't even care!

it just exists—
what the fuck!

i forgot about wanting to drive my car into a lake,
forgot about taxes,

just laughed at that bay leaf floating through soup
the way i was floating through life,

laughed because i promised to live
for something as stupid as a bay leaf.

interlude.

it seemed much later than it really was;
the sun had fallen asleep only a few minutes prior
but it felt like the darkness had come
ages ago.

we were dressed in denial in
the front seats of my camry at cool creek
with our feet up and spooky black playing.

we were attached always,
glued to the other's hip
giggling crying just being.

we talked about boys but
never needed them, and i
could face death or
even my parents
as long as i had you near.

i was the only one who
could ever thaw you and
you were the only one to ever hand me armor;

we dug up our oldest secrets and
told one another, spilled and melted
into the leather and i felt boneless
afterwards.

i wish i could hold onto
that feeling of you with me
but it's like trying to carry water in your
palms and i miss you terribly, always
always miss you terribly,
and without you
i still feel
hollow to this day.

defibrillation.

the way your voice cracked before you started to cry:
the eighth wonder of the world

i clung to you the way you clung to your seven-year smoking habit,
like to let go would be fatal.
you were rambling and intoxicated, face flushed

as you spilled drunk texts.
mascara waterfalling onto the sheets,
you told me you wanted to end it all

i went numb, as if you had reached into my lungs and
ripped out all of the oxygen there,
as if you had pulled the mattress out from underneath us

terribly terribly numb, i hung
suspended and weightless
in the pitch black of your bedroom

i didn't know what to say—
i still wonder what i could've said
could've done
besides lie there useless and unblinking
to make it alright for you

no one ever wants to talk about it and i was no different.

useless and hopeless and
curled up beside you, breathless—

how could i have breathed life into you
when i wanted to die too?

last night in noblesville.

there was a deep longing in my chest—
i ached to tell her about it
but i knew she wouldn't understand,
which caused a great divide within me.

she shuffled her feet, asked me why
i never tell her what's wrong anymore.
the entirety of the english language teetered on the edge of
    my tongue
but all that came out was

sorry.

i wasn't well-versed in expressing myself—
after all, how do you tell someone you love
that their presence is starting
to suck the life out of you?

i stared blankly
at the dwindling lamp behind her shoulder,
watched as the moths grew disinterested
and fluttered away.

sorry.

ok fine i miss you.

i whisper it to the lamp post,
the street, to anything and
anyone but
you.

to tell you would mean
an early death,
but that doesn't stop my
finger from lingering
over your name in my phone.

i find your face
in everything, i don't have to look hard
i just squint a bit and you're there
in the pavement the sky the walls.
all the time every morning every night.

in my dreams i find myself
at your doorstep with my arms open,
ready to bring you
home
even though i know
the consequences.
i wake up and remind myself that really,

the distance

is safer.

i go outside, it's pitch black and
i pace the empty cul-de-sac, i go in circles.
just like we used to do, go in
circles
circles
circles.

middle names.

a lot has changed since the last time we spoke.

i've seen my dad cry three times now
and my heart doesn't feel as heavy
when i bike past the movie theatre.

i drove around for hours the night after my birthday
and didn't think i was gonna make it home—
didn't want to make it home.

i wanted to show up at your old doorstep,
knock with the same hand
you used to seek out in the dark

but years from now we'll both
still be searching for something
feeling a little bit empty and a lot not-sure-why,

forgetting each other's middle names and
growing and cutting our hair
until we can't recognize ourselves.

i wish it could be like the movies,
wish we would find each other again and
talk like we used to without it killing us.

though i hope you're doing well,
it can take the universe a lot of convincing
to merge two disasters at once.

half-regrets.

there are too many people
i should've socked,
should've kissed,
should've spoken to.

too many times i wish i
would've learned to
love myself
despite looking like my mother.

veracity.

lounging in my left lung,
you whittled your signature
into some of the tissue there

a few times i considered eviction
thought maybe it wasn't healthy
to have you breathing for me all the time

i could never muster the courage—
or maybe it was just easier to pretend i was fine
carrying you and your dilemmas.

when you packed up and left,
i'll admit that the emptiness
was almost unbearable

and it hurt when it hit me
that i had never really been happy,
only distracted.

all the words that end in -mania.

there are days
i pull the hair
straight out of my head,
try to dig out the hurt
laying under my skin.
days i forget to breathe and
days i hoard the air around me.
i've thought about dying and
all its consequences,
compared it to the pain of
going on,
loving and hating
all different kinds of people,
making enough money
to survive but never enough to
thwart The Panic,
getting new jobs and
new bathroom stalls
to cry in.
i've pondered the labels
and prescriptions,
wondered how to survive
with a brain bent on
self-destruction and a body
that belongs to everyone but me.

pyrrhic victory.

trying to think of something to do—
some way to cope—
other than ignoring my friends
and picking my skin

instead of seeking out music
that will hurt my feelings,
or wasting my time on boys
who still have photos of their exes on their walls

but all of my memories are inside out
stuffed into drawers that can't close
and there isn't a corner in the world
that doesn't remind me of you.

note in chicago.

i left a note for you
somewhere deep in chicago
even though
i am almost certain
you'll never see it

but who knows—
maybe one day
you'll stumble around those same streets
drunk with your oxfords untied,
hair curly from the rain

trying to forget about us
and the love we made
as the world woke up
or the way your mom
disapproved of me
just the right amount

suddenly you'll trip,
stumble,
fall flat on your face—
splayed out and guffawing
until

you see a crumpled-up post-it
scuttle across the pavement
just slow enough
for you to read the great bold letters
i wrote when i thought it was love.

the last time i smoked.

waking up every morning
is just like driving into a fog

busy trying to forget that you love me because it hurts
feels kind of like running late
panicked and hurried and i'll-be-there-soon
rushing to meet you halfway

we both know the last voicemail i left you
i was high out of my mind
drained and drowning and held captive under the belief
    that i was dying
and as obsessed as i am with the idea,

that was the last time i smoked.

empty church parking lot.

when i visit here without you
i am colossally empty

like my passenger seat,
and the left half of my rib cage

like the air when your lips part to say something
but you decide to save your breath

i find myself drawn to that big old oak tree
the one that shielded us from rain and passerby

we used to splay our tattered jackets beneath it and lie there until
the darkness was stiff with silence and your mom called
    you home

we spoke about the moon and bank robberies,
about moving across the country and bad music,

but never really said what we wanted to

just let the words skate close to the edge of our tongues
before swallowing them whole and parting ways,
crossing our fingers that the other knew
 (i hope you knew)

vestigial responses.

i can't imagine i'm who you've been waiting for
when your fingers reach blindly for mine
my breath hitches as they intertwine
and you ask if your skin is cold—

but you're always warm
always a little too warm,
like you mean what you say
when you say you're in love

i can tell by the color in your cheeks
that when someone says they'll never hurt you
you have the grit to believe them—
and i wish i were like you

i wish i could believe something as
grandiose
and as
fatal
as that.

l*ve and its tendencies.

i never have seen myself
the way you tell me i should—
it is much easier to
ignore l*ve than to receive it.

after all, i've been given all kinds of
mixed messages about the thing. i don't know
if it's yelling kicking screaming or
giving up my body or
something more spiritual and
otherworldly than that. maybe
it's just chemical reactions or
maybe i was chiseled away at
until i fit perfectly next to you.
i don't know.

all i know is that there are times—
times when i consider
the sun an artist for creating
the perfect collage of freckles
on the bridge of your nose.

times i collect honey
from the hives in your eyes
and store it in a jar
on the highest shelf in my pantry
for safekeeping.

times i traverse through
the valleys in your palms and
hope to find my initials
written somewhere
in your future.
...is that l*ve?

never mind.

i don't need a word
for whatever it is
you stir up inside me.

i just know
it's as real as the pain
when you leave.

dissipate I.

no i don't want to open the door
i'd much rather slip beneath it
embrace the rug burns
and the splintering wood

i want to peel the bark away from a towering oak tree
step inside its hollow trunk and shut myself away
surrounded by the scent of sap and old tales
safe from the piercing winds and lethal cities

toxic questions and toxic people

dissipate II.

we're standing on the sun-soaked sidewalk barefoot
staring at the roof of a neighbor's house
and i'm not sure how to tell you
i'd rather claw beneath the shingles
than continue our one-sided conversation

i picture my bloody nails and scraped elbows
all worth it for the rush of relief
a fugitive beneath sleek grey planks
peeking out only to observe

decades passing,
my signature fading from important documents,
someone taking my phone number,
and the universe sleeping through
the last breath i take.

thoughts from the foot of my bed.

i thought the world would end when you left—
but here i am.

a little more fucked up, to be sure
but still here.

you know
i had a dream that everything happened the same

except this time you had the decency to say goodbye.
and as it turns out,

that was all i needed.

agnostic.

i love it all:

the nonsense you mutter in your sleep
your unkempt coffee-colored curls
your clean-shaven face
and our bodies bare beneath sheets

i only wish there were a way closer

the furrows in my fingerprints grasp at atoms
and intertwined limbs leave me longing still
 "god," darts past my lips

airy and weightless,
hurriedly expelled

not because i thought i might speak with him,

but because in the moment
i could fathom no other explanation.

i used to call my mom by her first name.

i went to a concert in downtown indianapolis—
spent thirty-five dollars for the ticket and
even more on gas,

only to stand frozen and sober in the crowd,
missing you
and who i wished you could be.

i turned down pills and poorly rolled blunts,
wishing that you would take me home,
tuck me in.

if i called you, could you hear me
over the deafening music, and
from across the chasm we had dug between us?

seizure-inducing lights,
perforated eardrums,
so many distractions—

but mom,
i am still so

empty.

love you more, love you most.

cigarettes and shoving and caffeine headaches
eyes like cold coffee, no sugar:

his words can be hard to swallow,
too bitter for my taste

he talks over my favorite songs,
keeps dirt trapped beneath his nails—

but i can't start my morning
without him.

unorthodox genie.

i won't stop driving until i run out of gas—
or i guess until i need to piss

i'll stay stuck on hague road
feeling wonderfully sorry for myself

wondering why none of my friends have messaged me,
then realizing i've put my phone on 'do not disturb'

a genie appears from one of the empty plastic water bottles
littering the floor of my car.

he slithers out with a purple aura and a shit-eating grin,
and asks for my three wishes,
but i only have two:

to drown my hippocampus in the lake off greyhound pass,
hold my writhing childhood memories under the murky
    water
until they go limp and cease to haunt me;

and that the chapstick in my center console wasn't melted.

is it considered minimalistic if i just want you?

i've been aching for simplicity:
an apartment barren of decoration
a little off-white room with a mattress on the hardwood
    floor
and a cranky AC tucked into the window

a TV but no batteries for its long-lost remote
and heavy hand-me-down comforters
not a lot of ingredients in the pantry
but enough to bake a poor excuse for a cake at two

no more disastrous, hopeless messes
except for the flour, and me, and you.

(sorry, i know you hate spiders.)

we get caught between
rushing to meet the day and

never stirring from the bed
we call ours.

we wrap each other in threads,
hold on so tight it's

a beautiful kind of smothering
that you never want to escape.

there's no greater joy than
spinning webs of

pink sheets and
rosy cheeks; i am

irrevocably in love and
i love to say so.

numbers divisible by three.

i know you love me
immensely, fully,
completely, but i still get nervous
sometimes that maybe
i'm too much to deal with. i think
it's because i've never had someone
watch me empty my tear ducts, watch me pace and
check the doorknob three, six,
thirty times
thirty-three times
and—
thirty-six times—
and still hold me at night like i am not
a mosaic of mascara tears and a ball of compulsions,
like i am everything they could ask for, love me like
i am worth more than the world, like
i don't drive them crazy
checking the doorknobs—
thirty-nine
forty-two
sixty-three times—

reversing amnesia.

there was a great pine tree in the front yard
its green needles flirted with the rain gutter

it nestled against the copper-colored bricks of my house, and
on windy nights it peeked into the second story bedroom window.

i took to hiding in the nook between that tree and those bricks,
making friends with the bottom of the trunk and its cantankerous branches

sometimes i brought allies to my sanctuary:
dandelions i had plucked from beneath the stop sign at the street corner
handfuls of helicopter seeds i collected off the sidewalk
a beaded bracelet tangled in our maple tree
crab apples i stole from our neighbors' clean-cut yard

i gathered them in a pile and told them everything about me,
about my parents' divorce and the cops that came,

but inevitably, they would wrinkle up
and stop contributing to the conversation.

so i'd travel to the backyard to recruit my dog—
my family could never agree on the spelling of her name
 (b-r-i-t-t-n-e-y).
we were a wonderful team—
i told her the few truths that i knew of the world
and she found squirrels to hassle.

when the snow came, i would suit up and
trek outside—wobble, really,
cushioned as a marshmallow,
with my dog in her booties and coat.

we'd plop on the ground,
slip our legs beneath a thick blanket of white,
and wait and wait,
hoping to freeze in place.

matryoshkas.

empty inside
and dark

whatever it is,
whatever it is

empty inside
yet compact

a million tiny emptinesses
stuffed within one another

dense, impossible
to wade through

empty inside
still tender

whatever it is,
whatever it is.

the corner of the room where my demon appears.

***

i still wake up sometimes
with him on top of me
one hand on my neck
and the other prying me open

doing things i can't talk about,
not in therapy or
to my closest friends or
even to myself most of the time

because of the fear that i might
drown in it
all over again, might be seized by it
at any given moment.

i made a list in my head
of all the things that i would
give up to forget about it, to have the memory of
his face and hands carved out of my

brain. i would shed my name, my
body, my life

to scrape him out.

and when i say i'm fine,
what i mean is that i am buried in water bills
from all the times
i have tried to wash the evil off.

a conversation between survivors.

***

seats leaned
way back,
necks craning
to the night sky.
phones on silent.
the lightest tap
of rain on the windshield.
you say nothing, but
there is an urgency in your voice,
tears standing on ledges.
i watch them each
as they jump.
i know that you
ache to hold and be held
if only he hadn't
made you fear touch.
i look away, know there
is nothing to say
and nothing to do
except roll my window down
and let the rain flood us too.

cinderblock.

a cinderblock loitered in my prefrontal cortex,
an ancient weight in my mind.

the red from the traffic lights dragged into thin lines,
and i was faintly aware of my tears

it became difficult to distinguish lanes from one another,
and i pulled over to collect myself,

watched my finger push the hazards on
and stared at the reflection in the rearview mirror.

i knew, sitting there in my car,
that i wasn't alone as i appeared to be;

there was a girl with messy bangs and porcelain skin
tugging at my sleeve and crying as hard as i wish i could

and i carried her on my back, heavy despite her size,
everywhere i went.

those panic attacks that seemed to grip me at random
didn't seem so random anymore—

like days ago when i had gone to the store,
and the ugly flickering ceiling lights started caving

and the aisles started collapsing

and the woman plucking a jar of applesauce from the top
   shelf sneered at me-

i realized it now:
all the while,

on my search for red bell peppers,
that little girl was pulling me into the white tile floor

beneath the dirt
and into the core of the earth

sitting in my car,
i realized it was just for some attention—

all for some attention.

all the times i had swatted her away,
worn short sleeves so she couldn't reach to tug at them

refused to meet her gaze in the mirror and avoided the
family photo albums,
came flooding back with a force that rendered me
   breathless

i reached into the passenger seat
grabbed her, put her in my lap,

and held both of us until we stopped crying—
and it took a while to stop crying.

she chipped away at the cinderblock in my brain,
put a small piece in her pocket to carry some of the weight

i said, *i do not know if anyone has ever apologized to you.*
and she shook her head.

my heart broke;
i told her i was sorry no one had ever said sorry

that no number of i-love-you's weighed as much as the hurt
that it had been too late the moment it had happened

for muting her, for putting her on hold
for making her endure that silence knowing

there is no greater prison sentence for a child
than to live through something like that and have no one
    to tell.

i said i was sorry i had not grown up to be the affirmation
she needed;
i promised to work on it.

she told me, in a small voice,
that she only wished i would hold her more.

so i promised to hold her more.

then i buckled her in
and i took us both home.

tiny.

i live in a compact box
taking up as little space as possible
and apologizing to those who see or hear me
my existence is so
minuscule that
sometimes,
i don't know
if i even
need
air.

blanket hoarding.

i hope you get enough time
to play out all the dreams
fighting for attention in your head
one by one, or maybe even twice over

i hope you get the chance
to see nooks and crannies in the world
so beautiful they steal your breath
and possess you to write again

i hope you return home one day
not heartbroken that life slipped through your fingers
but grateful you were able to grasp anything at all
with your spirit quiet, warm, at ease

i hope you slip into your bed
without the space hurting
and you hog all the blankets
like you deserve—

like you've always deserved.

bathtub in flames.

***

it's hard to say what happened for sure.
your brain shuts down
when things are too horrific to live through.

but your body stores the memories,
pries your skin open and shoves the hurt
in a bed of muscle and

somewhere down the line,
whether it's months or decades later,
the seed crawls from its plot, climbs into your brain.

you never really forget.

the icy tiles beneath my feet
and the hum of the bathroom fan
all seem miles away.

his hands go where
they don't belong, and
i am set on fire—

nerves melting and numb,
my mind turning to ash,
i burn alive to escape the pain.

i know there was a lot going on—
with the divorce, and work.
life gets busy.

but i would have given up
anything in this world
for you to notice the bathtub in flames.

strangulation.

***

i can't kept my mouth shut
i want it off my chest
it's suffocating and
debilitating
holding my breath
because he touched me
and told me
not to tell but
i want it off my chest!
it is suffocating—

and i will
not
let it kill me.

how i wish the conversation would go.

***

nobody knows how to respond
when you tell them something that isn't pretty.

they get awkward, shift around in their seat
and look for distractions,

try to bring up new movies,
ask about your plans for the holidays.

i wish i could take them out to dinner
and just say it,

yes, yes, i was molested; it went on for years.
can i get a refill?

they wouldn't claw away from the topic,
wouldn't break and need holding.

they'd nod, *ahh* and *mhm*,
twirl their wine around in their glass,

sitting an arm's length away
with a thoughtful look on their face.

they don't ask me *who? when?*
or *how many times?*

they let me hurt and breathe
in peace,

just say *that must have been horrible—you know,
i went to school with someone who was molested...*

and the waiter comes back,
says *so sorry that happened to you*

and refills
my glass.

the pause.

i find myself here many times throughout
the seasons, just sitting as the car runs
with my knees tight, glued to my chest so that
nothing can move me. i am lost again
and it's not the type of thing you can just check a map for,
i mean i am lost in a colossal way,
juggling the responsibility of being loved and
wanting to die so intensely that it blinds me sometimes,
so that's why i pull over.
i swear it just finds me,
it slips between my fingers and
up my arms into my ears and chokes my brain.
i hide and i don't move, if i don't move it can't see me,
i'm not alive or here and
nobody knows me or stops to get to know me.
i exist but only barely,
and that's the greatest thing, this Pause:
where the world is still going on and no one is sad but
also no one is asking me about my bills or my sexuality,
i wish that it could be this way all the time.
i wish everyone would forget my name or
i wish that i didn't have such a rotten brain, maybe things
would be different.
but they aren't, so i find myself here,
the side of the road, throughout the year
crying quietly and
clinging to The Pause.

on humans and addiction.

you go barreling backwards sometimes,
headfirst, without meaning to
back to the things that kill you

you take up smoking again
take blades to your skin
just to slice through the numbness,
or maybe to provide an exit where the
feeling might slip out of you.

the feeling that you

talk talk talk about

but can never evict.

it floods your lungs like pneumonia
and you can't breathe well because of it;

it welds to your organs, pours into the crevices of your heart
and swells there,
swells until you think you might burst and
you have to leave parties to calm yourself.

it wedges itself so deep you have to wonder if it isn't just
meant to be a part of you.

posthumous apology.

my childhood home is abandoned and flooded
and that feels pretty appropriate,

considering the years that separate me from it now
and the things that happened there.

i only hope that,
though the furniture's drowning,

our ghosts can
live comfortably.

our souls as sponges.

people devastate each other and move on
and it may never make sense to me;

i suppose there are some things that our souls just
aren't meant to absorb.

i lie awake sometimes, cradling one hand
in the smooth palm of the other

watching my belly rise and fall
listening to the earth move

i try to distract myself, i think about how
i need to get new batteries for the clock but

the safety of morning always feels so far away.

that late-night regret crawls beneath my skin and settles there;
if it left me alone, i think maybe i could breathe

but i have to go through hell and two pills
just for fifteen minutes of sleep

so instead i lay there,
unblinking, thinking that

there are hands that hurt
and hands that heal,

and we decide which we have
and the world spins and we die.

water over white stones.

it's not even 5 a.m.
yet i slip from your embrace

slowly, so the bed doesn't creak,
and tuck the blanket under your chin.

i flip the *cigarettes after sex* vinyl onto its other side
and tiptoe out of our bedroom,

into the kitchen where my bare feet skate across tiles
bordered with sandwich crumbs and rolling paper,

and muted light dances across un-muddied snow
from the night before.

the finches have flocked south for the winter,
and neighbors hush their alarm clocks with heavy hands,

but i am wide awake
and grateful

thinking about all the nights
you spent kissing sense into me,

and when you took my hands downtown,
your hair at war with the wind,

to tell me for the first time
that you loved me;

it erased years of wondering
and terrible aching to know

i belong in the world;
i belong in your arms.

neon turmoil.

every other weekend is
an assortment
of takeout boxes, of
fuck-ups and
emotions i bury deep, emotions
that come out only when i get drunk
and always
with such a vengeance
that they knock me to the floor.
i've cried more times than i can count
in the church parking lot by the strip,
cried about all sorts of things
with neon lights swimming in my tears,
cried about things my mom has told me and
cried about losing my keys.
just all the stupid things that
make me human,
all of the things that mean
i am miserable but alive—

at least i am still alive.

empty buckets for eyes.

i don't want to know
how many hours of my life
i've spent laying in my driveway
staring at the night sky
with empty buckets for eyes.
it would devastate me.
things seem so meaningless already;
why ask me about my nine to five
or what i had for dinner?
i choke on
every passing minute,
waste time calculating
how much time i've wasted
fixing bad parking jobs,
sleeping through alarms,
and worrying over loose ends
that don't matter
to anyone outside
this tiny galaxy.

day two hundred ten.

i wake up.
it's already late;
the sun has crawled
from the center of the sky
and is still sinking.
my room is blanketed
in a muted darkness;
everything is fuzzy
and swirling.
i inch a foot out
from under the blankets,
test the air—
fucking cold!—
and retreat again.
think about the mail
i have to ship out,
the drawers on my dresser
that i ought to clean and close,
the medicine i forgot to take
last night,
the messages that
i have yet to reply to.
i close my eyes.
go back to sleep.

past the popcorn ceiling.

***

there are times i have to reach out,
touch my stained-glass skin,
just to be certain that i'm really here.

it's a hard thing to be sure of
when you exist in two places
at once:

a hell tucked between
where i am now
and where i used to be.

i try repeating what i know in my head:
i'm twenty-one, i'm safe,
i'm in bed.

but still i get stuck sometimes,
can't move can't scream,
stuck in between

my thighs cold and
his hands colder.
five years old,

trying to float out of my
body, past the popcorn ceiling,
past the roof the trees, float

out of
his

reach.

i'm twenty-one,
i'm safe,
i'm in bed.

i try to bring myself back,
try to wiggle my toes
recall the date or scrunch my eyes

try to picture the sun and the moon
or my neighbor who leaves
the same time every night

but

i'm stuck just staring,
unmoving,
at the ceiling,

feeling five again
with no way
to wrench myself out.

beacon park drive.

i melt, like liquid glass
between the cracks
in my old wooden deck.

lie with my spine
flush against the earth and
look up through the strips of dandelion light

the things that haunted me
now drift by on gentle breezes,
at peace and flowing without fighting

the fury hushes,
and the guilt too. it all
comes to rest like autumn leaves,

never to be disturbed
by a gust of wind again,
never to bloom on another branch.

my heels sink and the world
cradles my head as my eyes close,
i can

hear the *click click click*
of my first dog's paws against the planks
and the patter of my younger self's bare feet.

i smile

and i do not startle
when the rubble shifts to take me in,
or when the earth nudges me and sighs:

welcome home.

fearless as the sand.

the sand doesn't go up in arms when the tide takes it home

so no,

i am not afraid to die

not afraid

to float weightlessly between stars,

conscious only of the fact that i am

burning

dying

and visible to someone.

cataracts.

i almost felt like myself this morning
the sky was splitting, just opening
its cobalt curtains.
i was thinking about
all of the things my dad sacrificed that i
didn't appreciate as a kid and
the blurry line between sister and mother,
mother and sister.
about my brothers
and the spacious, claustrophobic world and
finding my own place somewhere.

i considered
all the times i've ever wanted to die,
and clutched at the times i never want
to forget. it's true that
Happiness cowers
and does not show her face
very often to me,
but still i seek and believe.
blind and scrambling in the dark,
feeling the walls with my palms
trying to get to her even
if only for a brief,
fleeting
conversation,
an exchange of hello's or even
shy glances. just to

know her again for a moment and
to have that to hold onto.

i almost felt like myself this morning.
the sun peeled my blinds back and
peeked in and
there was Happiness, the flighty thing,
sitting at the foot of my bed with
eyes full of promise.
i offered my hand to her and
pulled my lips
into a smile;
like swimming during a storm,
i know the risk but i
still try.

grow up!

the moon doesn't care

if you don't wear makeup

or if you slam the door to make a point

and neither does your boyfriend.

telephone poles.

i always wanted to avoid
being a flowery poet
who spoke of love and hearts swelling—

but it is impossible to escape it
now that i've met
you.

i ache to make playlists
stuffed full of love songs
and saccharine melodies,

dedicate my life to
melting into you
and your gravelly voice.

sometimes, i could swear
the only things holding the sky up
are telephone poles and you.

occasionally, even the wires snap,
colliding in a frenzy of fireworks
to the ground,

but there is always you.
and i hope that it
will always be you.

reruns.

***

some days my nerves
go on strike, turn off.

other times, they shatter
at the slightest touch.

everything is always
too much or nothing at all,

i am either here so much it hurts
or so gone i don't need a name—

even though it happened years ago,
it still happens every night.

120 bpm.

why do you do it,
this pacing back and forth?

this going, and worrying,
and wondering.

can't you sit with yourself for two minutes,
or does it frighten you?

you can't know where you're going
or if you'll get there on time.

you aren't sure, never have been,
always will be—unsure

so just sit.

let it be uncertain and
terrifying,

give it some time to engulf you
so that you may also be released.

the cycle.

***

that's how it goes:
you think the wound has closed,
but a night always comes
when you can think of little else
besides the torment he passed onto you.
and you have to wonder if someone hurt him
before he hurt you
or if the bastard was just born
with no fucking empathy.

catharsis.

***

it doesn't hurt like it used to:
that rawness, like your skin after
being kissed by a cigarette,
does heal after a time.

i stormed back to the house
the exact place where he
took my body from me,
and met him in my mind,

seething. i tried to
drown him in alcohol, tried to
cut him out, tried to
suffocate him with sleep.

but nothing saves you after
you have been held hostage
in your own body, except to
look that silhouette in the eyes

and allow the tears to

flow
flow
flow

for years, maybe decades,
until you are able to
cut the cord cuffing you to him and
let him plunge, with his filthy hands,

to hell.

be patient.

***

this shit is non-linear and,
though it's very disorderly,
i am at peace with it

the type of peace that good men
and dogs exhibit just before
they die

sometimes the memories devour my cells,
toss me to my bedroom floor and
i don't get up for hours

i don't exist, i forget to
eat, i close my window and i don't want
to be seen. i want

to disintegrate,
melt into the floorboards
and never be touched again.

i have to remind myself where i am, my age,
to remember that he isn't here and
he can't hurt touch reach me

i get so angry about it,
i can't help but think
of destroying myself.

but there are other days still
that i am able to exist
much in the way i did before:

days where all of the fear and shame
pour out of my palms
as if they had never intended to ruin me in the first place

relief floods me the way wine floods the veins;
without even realizing it,
i take shelter in my body

and live again.

acknowledgments.

There are countless spiral notebooks, half-full of gibberish, stowed away in my closet in a box labeled "Memories." I grew up documenting my life in poems, trying to keep track of my experiences and to tell my story to a nonexistent audience. These poems have allowed me, as an adult, to reflect on my roots and connect with my inner child, which inspired *bathtub in flames*.

This collection never would have come to fruition, however, without the other inspirations in my life.

First, thank you to my wonderful dad, Troy, and stepmom, Kirsten, for loving me as I've tried (and failed) to do many different things and be many different people. Your unwavering compassion and support keep me going.

Thank you to my goofy and ambitious brothers, Brayten, Brennan, and Dillon, and to my wild and beautiful sister, Sarah. You guys are the highlight of my life.

Thank you to my friends, specifically Deidra Alexandrea, who came to me when I needed her most and is the best friend that anyone could ask for (even though we can never decide where to eat). Thank you to Zahra Fawkes for being a beautiful human and helping me become the woman that I am today; to Isabella Palacios for sending me pictures of frogs and comforting me in the late hours of the night; to Katelyn Gossard for keeping the group chat in tears and accepting my craziness; to Nicole Robinson for roasting my exes and being my hockey buddy; to Ally Campbell for putting up with my long rants and being one of the most compassionate people I know; to Abbey Luna for being my first best friend and growing with me to this day; to Reade Kessler for loving me fully.

Thank you to the team at New Degree Press. Thank you to Elissa Graeser, my developmental editor (and the first person to read my poetry), who reminded me why I had to keep going; to Emily Price, my revisions editor, who helped me improve my poems in ways I never imagined; to the design team, including Gjorgji Pejkovski and Josip Perić, who brought my book cover to life; to Matt Phillips and my other editors, who dotted the i's and crossed the t's; to Leila Summers, Brian Bies, and Eric Koester for making this opportunity possible.

Finally, thank you to everyone who supported me by pre-ordering a copy of this book. Your kind words inspired me throughout the process of writing, and I will forever be grateful that you saw worth in my work.

www.ingramcontent.com/pod-product-compliance
Lightning Source LLC
LaVergne TN
LVHW011841060526
838200LV00054B/4125